Poop Detectives
Working Dogs in the Field

Ginger Wadsworth

Pips rests after a long day in the field.

To Dr. Walter M. Boyce and Dr. Winston Vickers, wildlife veterinarians with the University of California, Davis

In memory of Rich Guadagno, manager at Baskett Slough National Wildlife Refuge, Oregon, where scat-detection dogs searched successfully for Kincaid's lupine. Rich Guadagno died on 9/11/2001 in Pennsylvania on Flight 93.

Text copyright © 2016 by Ginger Wadsworth
Photographs copyright © by individual photographers
Photographs on back cover (lower left and upper right) and pages 2, 12, 12–13, 13, 14, 15, 16, 17, 18, 27 (right), 28, 30, 31, 32, 41, 42, 42–43, 54–55, 60, 61, 63, 64, 67, 69, 70, 72, 75, and 80 copyright © University of Washington. Used with permission. Developed by the Center for Conservation Biology/Conservation Canines.
Charlesbridge and colophon are registered trademarks of Charlesbridge Publishing, Inc.

Published by Charlesbridge, 85 Main Street, Watertown, MA 02472
(617) 926-0329 • www.charlesbridge.com

Library of Congress Cataloging-in-Publication Data
Wadsworth, Ginger, author.
Poop detectives: working dogs in the field/by Ginger Wadsworth.
    pages cm
ISBN 978-1-58089-650-4 (reinforced for library use)
ISBN 978-1-60734-767-5 (ebook)
ISBN 978-1-60734-650-0 (ebook pdf)
1. Working Dogs for Conservation—Juvenile literature. 2. Detector Dogs—Training—Juvenile literature.
3. Working dogs—Training—Juvenile literature. 4. Detector dogs—Juvenile literature. I. Title.
SF428.75.W33 2016
636.7'0886—dc23   2015026876

Printed in China
(hc) 10 9 8 7 6 5 4 3 2 1

Display type set in Khaki, designed by Aerotype
Text type set in Adobe Caslon Pro
Color separations by Colourscan Print Co Pte Ltd. in Singapore
Printed by 1010 Printing International Limited in Huizhou, Guangdong, China
Production supervision by Brian G. Walker
Designed by Whitney Leader-Picone and Susan Mallory Sherman

Title page: Tia and her handler, Alice Whitelaw, search for kit foxes in the Central Valley, California.

Table of Contents

Nitro leads his handler to some scat in the snow.

Introduction
A New Job for Freddie?

As a puppy Freddie had so much energy that his owner couldn't handle him. Even with a daily run, Freddie managed to chew slippers, destroy a sofa, and nudge open kitchen cabinets and scatter the contents all over the apartment while his owner was at work.

Freddie, a border-collie mix whose ancestors loved nothing more than to run full-speed around a flock of sheep and herd them into a pen, was miserable in a tiny apartment. His sad yet desperate owner turned him in to the local animal shelter with a suggestion. Maybe someone who owned a ranch could adopt and love the wiry dog with the chocolate-brown eyes.

For days Freddie paced in his pen, wearing down his toenails and losing weight. Family after family toured the shelter in search of the right dog or cat. No one wanted Freddie. Shelter employees feared he would have to be put to sleep.

Abandoned dogs of all sizes and ages crowd animal shelters across the United States.

Left: This dog waits at a shelter for someone to adopt him.

Playing the Game

Finding that perfect poop-sniffing pooch isn't easy. "The dog needs to be able to sit and behave on command, but it also needs to have a wild, curious spirit," says wildlife biologist and dog trainer Alice Whitelaw.

Whitelaw and other trainers agree that detection dogs are fearless, spirited, and athletic animals. They are typically lean in build and hyper-focused. When their work switch is on, they have extreme drive, and they want to "win the game." As Dr. Katherine Ralls, a conservation biologist, says, "They're obsessive-compulsive dogs. They want to play with a Frisbee 24 hours a day."

Or in Freddie's case, a bright yellow tennis ball!

One morning a dog trainer walked into the shelter. She worked in the field with wildlife biologists and their **canine** assistants. One of her dogs was retiring, and the trainer was looking for a replacement. The perfect dog for the job would have to:

- Follow orders
- Be tough, energetic, and adventurous
- Find things that are nearly impossible to see
- Ride in a crate in the back of a truck
- Run long distances
- Be a fast learner
- Be obsessed with toys

The trainer visited many local shelters looking for the right dog. She knew the statistics. Less than 1 percent of all dogs qualify to become a detection canine.

She strolled up and down the rows of dog pens. While casually studying each dog, she bounced a yellow tennis ball. Dogs barked and bayed, pawed the wire cages, and whined for a friendly hand and a pat. Only one dog followed the tennis ball, his eyes never straying from the yellow orb. Every bit of Freddie's body tensed. He wanted that ball more than anything! And that was exactly what the trainer was looking for—a dog with the drive to work relentlessly for a special reward, like the tennis ball.

That day Freddie left the dog shelter with the dog trainer. He pranced to her pickup, carrying the tennis ball in his mouth. Freddie had been rescued from certain death, and now he had a chance to begin a new life. He was about to

start an intense training program. If successful, he would join an elite group of dogs that travel the world sniffing for wildlife **scat**, urine, horns, and hair—and sometimes the animals themselves.

Freddie had a chance to make a career change, as trainers sometimes call it. He wasn't a good pet. Would he succeed at his new job?

Nothing tastes yummier than a saliva-soaked tennis ball!

1 The Nose Knows
The Science Behind Super Sniffers

Olfaction, the process of smelling, is a dog's primary sense. Inside a dog's nose are some two hundred million smell-receptor **cells**—more than thirty times the number in our human noses. Dogs can smell multiple layers of chemicals, or scents, at one time. We can't. Imagine a pot of chili bubbling on the stovetop. In the next room a dog inhales and exhales quickly, drawing more of the scent inside its nose. These smells might draw the dog into the kitchen, where it continually takes tiny sniffs. The dog can smell all the ingredients separately: tomatoes, chili powder, beans, onions, ground beef, and more.

These scents, or smells, cannot be seen or photographed. They cannot be identified like fingerprints. They cannot be analyzed in a scientific laboratory, either. But dogs can find them—and tell precisely what they are.

Their incredible sense of smell makes dogs uniquely qualified for all kinds of detection work.

You've Got P-Mail!
Dogs love to sniff pee-soaked trees and posts, and poop left by other dogs. They are checking their p-mail to get messages. We don't know exactly what the messages say, but we do know that dogs leave some kind of information behind for their buddies when they pee or poop.

Left: Sniff, sniff, sniff . . . each smell tells this dog a story.

Some dogs work at airports and train stations, sniffing suitcases, bags, and boxes for drugs or even for fruits or vegetables that may contain unwanted insects.

Dog Detectives

Most dogs are pets, but many others are working dogs. **Canine handlers** guide and train them for careers in different fields. There are police dogs, guard dogs, hunters, sled dogs, farm dogs, and service dogs that are trained to assist people with disabilities.

There is also a small but fast-growing category of four-legged super sniffers. Some dogs learn to smell life-threatening changes in a diabetic person's blood-sugar level. They alert the person by barking so he or she will know to take insulin. Some dogs can detect changes in a person with epilepsy before he or she has a seizure. Dogs can smell some kinds of cancers in the human body, too.

After a catastrophe like an earthquake or explosion, canine detectors clamber over the rubble to locate bodies and trapped survivors. They also work with police officers and search-and-rescue teams to search for lost hikers in the mountains.

And then there are the poop detectives.

"The Guru of Doo-Doo"

Many wildlife scientists rely on the **data,** or information, they collect from animals that have been caught in traps. The animals are knocked out with tranquilizer darts, fitted with **Global Positioning System (GPS)** collars, then released. It is challenging, time-consuming work.

There is always the risk that trapped or tranquilized animals will go into shock and die. Traps must be checked regularly so that captured animals don't die from lack of food and water, or from exposure to extreme temperatures.

Dr. Samuel Wasser wanted to develop ways to study wildlife populations in a safer, noninvasive way. Starting in the mid-1980s, he and other scientists at the Center for Conservation Biology at the University of Washington began examining animal scat—also called **excrement**, poop, droppings, **feces**, **dung**, or fecal matter. Scat comes in different sizes, shapes, and textures. Bear scat is usually loose and contains some plant material; tiger scat has hair and bone fragments. Whale poop is gooey. Whatever its appearance, scat can give scientists a broad picture of the distribution and health of many **species** of wild animals without actually seeing or disturbing them.

Unfortunately, it takes a long time for a human to find and collect scat. Some scat, like that of a grizzly bear, is large, but spread out across a vast **territory**. Some scat, like that of a fisher (a type of weasel) is much smaller—about the size of a house cat's poop. Imagine trying to find little pieces of scat in the dense forests where the fisher lives!

Dr. Wasser wondered if he could somehow train dogs that sniff for drugs to help find scat instead. Maybe the scat collecting would go more quickly. In 1997 he contacted Sergeant Barbara Davenport, the lead narcotics-dog trainer at Washington State's Department of Corrections. He asked her if dogs could be trained to find scat.

Sergeant Davenport was open to Dr. Wasser's idea. So Wasser screened hundreds of dogs at various animal shelters and adopted several candidates. Under Davenport's supervision, biologists from the University of Washington began to work side by side with prison guards and police officers to train dogs.

Air Scenting

Bloodhounds and similar kinds of tracking dogs do not make good scat-detection dogs. They tend to keep their nose to the ground to smell skin cells that have fallen off a target.

Wildlife scientists prefer dogs that "air scent," picking up the "thread" of an odor as it blows away from its source, much like a trail of campfire smoke. When these breeds are working, they move their bodies, tails, and heads back and forth, constantly taking in small sniffs of air. Labradors, German shepherds, border collies, Australian cattle dogs, and mixes of these breeds are good "air scenters."

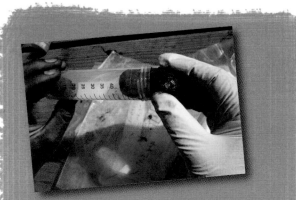

Stories from Scat

After a dog finds a scat, its handler collects the poop and sends it to a laboratory. Technicians look at the **DNA** in the scat, which tells a story about the animal.

DNA stands for deoxyribonucleic acid. It is in every cell of every single animal and plant. We humans have trillions upon trillions of cells in our bodies. Each cell has a job: to aid eyesight, carry oxygen, help digest food, and more. DNA tells the cells what to do.

DNA tests, along with other lab tests, such as checking for **parasites**, can tell a scientist many things: what an animal has been eating and drinking, if it is sick or stressed, how old the animal is, how far it has traveled, and whether it is male or female. As Dr. Wasser says, "You can get a lot of information on a species without ever seeing a single animal."

Then Wasser and his team began to train their dogs to sniff for animal scat—specifically grizzly and black-bear scat. The handlers had to be trained, too! They had to get physically fit and learn to bound over the moss-covered forest floor. They also needed to recognize and respond to their dogs' split-second behavior changes—speeding up at the scent of a target, acting confused because the wind shifted, or balking at crossing a river that looked too deep.

Two years after approaching Davenport for advice, Wasser completed his first major field study using canine detectors. The dogs, with their highly developed sense of smell, accomplished much more than humans could—in a shorter amount of time and with less impact on the environment and the animal being studied. The evidence from the collected scat provided a snapshot of the number of bears in a two-thousand-square-mile area, what they were eating, and much more.

Today Dr. Wasser is recognized as the pioneer of the scat-detection field and the "Guru of Doo-Doo." His bear study firmly launched the Center for Conservation Biology's canine program—also called the Conservation Canines program—which now trains and sends dog teams on assignments around the world.

For every potential scat-detection dog, it all begins with school!

Lessons Learned

Dr. Wasser and his team learned some valuable lessons from their work with the first group of detection dogs. First of all, they had to adjust to doing field research in a new way, by relying on a four-legged assistant. Second, they discovered the importance of developing a strong relationship with the dog. And third, they realized that the dog had to be obsessed, or even a bit crazed, over one special thing, like a ball or a pull toy. Immediately rewarding the dog with the ball or toy for a well-done job was essential.

Left: After his successful bear study, Samuel Wasser went on to work with many canine detectives, including Tucker the whale dog.

2 School Is in Session
Training a Scat-Detection Dog

Every working dog goes to school. Classes can be held in a canine training center, in a room in a community center, in a field, or even in someone's backyard. Dogs usually graduate after several months, but there's no right or wrong amount of time.

The key is practice, practice, practice. Instructors make the dogs repeat tasks over and over again. After the dogs learn to identify one kind of scat, they are introduced to new scents. The "students" earn lots of rewards: praise, tasty treats, and time to play with toys. During breaks, they rest, drink water, or romp with their canine buddies.

There can even be final exams! Barbara Davenport, the sergeant who helped Samuel Wasser train his first detection dogs, now heads PackLeader, a canine training center in Washington. She expects all dogs and handlers to pass a certification test before going into the field.

But how do you actually train a super sniffer?

Sometimes classes can happen on the water. Here, Gator is learning to track floating whale scat.

Left: All eyes are on the boss—Heath Smith!
Or is it the red ball that has everyone's attention?

Trainers and Trainees

Most of the dogs at Dr. Wasser's Center for Conservation Biology were adopted from animal-rescue and shelter organizations when they were one and a half to three years old. Because of their extra-high energy, these dogs didn't make successful pets.

At the Center for Conservation Biology, dogs can breathe clean mountain air, get top-notch food, and train with handlers who want them to succeed.

In their new lives the dogs live at a training facility in the University of Washington's 4,300-acre Pack Forest Center for Sustainable Forestry in the foothills of Mount Rainier. The barnlike main building has indoor-outdoor kennels for thirty dogs.

Each handler is typically involved in the training and care of two or three dogs. According to Wasser, being a dog handler isn't a job, but a lifestyle. A trainer goes where his or her dogs are needed, for as long as is needed. But not everyone has experience working in remote wilderness areas or is willing to be separated from friends and family for several months. It takes commitment, sacrifice, and time.

Many trainers start out as volunteers while studying at the University of Washington. The volunteers maintain the facility, assist in the field, help with the landscaping, and exercise the dogs. Working with lots of dogs is a good way to find out if being a trainer and handler is the right job for you.

School Days

The dogs get breakfast at 7 a.m. Then they walk or jog with their handlers. They spend the rest of the day going over practice problems until dinnertime.

Each dog must learn **scenting**—how to search for and identify a smell. The trainer's goal is to teach the dog to find one smell—the scat of a specific type of animal—and to ignore all other odors.

Handlers first use scent containers in a training area. Hidden in some of them is the target scat—about one fourth cup of it. The others hold "distractions"—strong-smelling substances such as toothpaste or perfumed lotion. The trainer introduces the target scent to the dog. Then he or she takes the dog past each scent container. When the dog reaches the scat, it reacts with leaps, twirls, and excited barks, then sits. In dog-training lingo, this is called **indicating** or **alerting**. The dog is immediately rewarded.

The next phase takes the team into a practice field, an area that might be the size of a football field. The trainer has placed the target scat somewhere in the field. It's time for the dog to find it.

The dog runs. The handler directs the dog using word commands, body language, and hand signals:

- Go Left
- Go Right
- Stop
- Come

Total trust between dog and handler is essential!

Scent containers might be open jars, hollowed-out cement blocks, or specially made boxes. Here, jars hang below the tabletop. One of them contains the target scent. But which one is it?

Even with their keen noses, dogs like Winnie need training to find specific scat— especially when it's small, like this fisher poop.

Graduation

After successful trials in the practice field, the dog is ready to locate scat in the wild. Dog and handler might be sent to the mountains, grasslands, desert, forest, or other **habitat**.

Success—and failure—in the field depend on many factors, including the size of the scat and the territory of the **target animal**. Tiny scat and a large, dense territory can make the search more difficult.

Rain and wind can also be problems. Rain can wash away scat. Erratic wind currents can confuse and frustrate a dog. "If the wind blows around [the scat] in a circle, the dog may run around in a circle, too," says Dr. Wasser.

Whatever the conditions, the trainer knows to act quickly and decisively, commanding the dog to keep it focused on the search. The team has already practiced these commands many times in school.

Star Student: Wicket

Working Dogs for Conservation, a nonprofit organization based in Three Forks, Montana, worked with Wasser and Davenport to help create the field of canine scat detection. Its goal, according to co-founder Aimee Hurt, is for a wildlife biologist "to be able to count on a competent detection-dog team, as well as have reasonable expectations for what the team will be able to accomplish."

When Hurt adopted Wicket, a Labrador mix, from a shelter, employees there told her that Wicket was crazy and that she wouldn't make a good family pet.

And they were right, Hurt recalls. Wicket has off-the-charts energy, so Hurt runs her in the woods, hoping to tire her out. Sometimes Wicket might sit for hours by a water spigot, waiting for someone to turn it on so she can chase the stream. "She'll wait quietly, but shiver with anticipation while we water the garden before her turn."

Wicket is also smart and eager to learn. Hurt first trained Wicket to locate globs of hair gel, which is "pungent enough for a dog to detect from a distance." Wicket then astonished Hurt by learning to identify many types of scat right away. Within a few months Hurt was ready to put her "crazy" rescue dog into the field.

Today Wicket can find twenty-six (and counting) different scents.

Left: No soft, squishy toys for Wicket! Her ball, made of sturdy rubber, gets a daily workout.

Going Back to School

Dr. Todd Steury, a professor at Auburn University in Alabama, studies threatened and endangered **carnivores** in southern parts of the United States, as well as invasive pythons in Florida's Everglades National Park. After hearing about Dr. Wasser's work, Professor Steury wondered if trained canines could help his team collect data, too.

Steury contacted Auburn University's Canine Detection Research Institute, a training facility where dogs learn to sniff for bombs, drugs, and bodies. Admitting that he was more of a cat person than a dog person, Dr. Steury asked the staff about "the possibility of training a dog to find scat." He added that the dogs would live at the university's veterinary school and get the best possible medical care and training.

An EcoDogs handler signals Bishop to sit and wait beside a pile of bear scat.

The professor expected them to laugh at his request. Instead, he recalls, "They looked at me kind of funny, but in the end, they said, 'Yeah, we can do it.'" Dr. Steury acquired several trained dogs that could detect bombs. They just needed to be redirected to become ecological detection dogs.

That's how EcoDogs: Detection Dogs for Ecological Research was born.

ooo

Pepin plays tug-of-war with his handler after a successful training session in the field.

Owning a detection dog isn't easy or cheap. According to Aimee Hurt, having a detection dog is a "24–7 endeavor. Lifelong, from training to retirement." But it's worth it to Hurt, Steury, and other trainers. Once trained, their four-legged search partners will do whatever is asked of them for nothing more than a treat, some water, and "the love of the people at the end of their leashes."

3 Into the Wild
Gathering Grizzly Scat

One of the most challenging assignments a scientist can get is grizzly tracking. Grizzly bears roam millions of acres, so it can be hard to find them or their scat. Studying them is also hazardous work. They are big and unpredictable, and they can run as fast as thirty-five miles an hour. No scientist wants to stumble across an angry grizzly bear in the field.

But studying them is important. In 1975, grizzly bears were declared an **endangered species**. At that time there were only eight hundred to one thousand grizzlies in the continental United States. Although they have been making a slow comeback since then—and are no longer on the endangered-species list—it has taken decades for their population to recover. To make sure the bears continue to increase in numbers, wildlife biologists are monitoring their health and well-being.

Left: Good boy! Dr. Ngaio Richards of Working Dogs for Conservation confirms that Orbee has found grizzly-bear poop.

Bear Bells Ring

Detection dogs are amazingly smart and brave. Most dogs would get one whiff of bear scat, turn, and run. Not Orbee! He sweeps back and forth across remote backcountry, jumping downed trees with his nose high and his mouth wide open. He wears jangly bells on his collar to alert bears that unfamiliar activity (human and dog) is nearby.

Once while Orbee and his owner, Aimee Hurt, were passing a thicket of willows in Alaska, Orbee acted odd. Hurt could see it in the way her dog held and moved his body. They were in bear country, so Hurt immediately directed Orbee to come to her side, and then they quickly walked away. Looking back, Hurt saw a grizzly standing on its hind legs, watching them. She figured that Orbee smelled the grizzly—and the curious bear just wanted a peek at them! Orbee was wearing bear bells, but Hurt isn't too sure they made any difference.

Not Just Bears

Most wildlife-detection dogs are trained to recognize the scat of many different animals. Wicket, for example, can locate black-bear, wolf, mountain-lion, and gorilla scat, as well as grizzly poop. She also searches for the scat of fishers (see below), a forest-dwelling relative of the weasel. In the early part of the twentieth century, fishers were trapped almost to **extinction** for their soft, silky coats. Today they are still rare in the Rocky Mountains. Aimee Hurt, Samuel Wasser, and other wildlife biologists want to know why the fishers are disappearing.

They also want to know why the number of porcupines in the area is increasing. Was it the early **poaching** of the fishers, which **prey** on porcupines? Now that the porcupines are more prevalent, they are causing substantial forest damage. When one animal species, like the fisher, is in decline, the **balance of nature** goes out of kilter.

To Cage or Not to Cage

Researchers often use baited wire cages to temporarily capture wild animals. To attract bears, they might place a salmon carcass or some wild berries inside the trap. A hungry bear walks in, and the cage door snaps shut behind it. Then the scientists shoot the bear with a non-lethal tranquilizer dart. The carefully aimed shot inserts a needle into the bear, and the team waits until the drug paralyzes the animal. The next steps—listening to the bear's heart and lungs; looking at its teeth, claws, and skin; and drawing blood samples—are important but dangerous. What if the drug wears off?

There's another problem with baited cages: they can lead to incomplete data. Samuel Wasser's team at the Center for Conservation Biology discovered that only male bears tend to amble into baited cages. Not females, especially those with cubs.

So wildlife biologists are turning to detection dogs because they can find the scat of all the target animals: males, females, and cubs. The information from the bears' scat reveals where they are and how they are doing in the wild, without disturbing them or putting scientists in harm's way.

"Go Find It, Camas!"

Alice Whitelaw is a wildlife biologist who has always been surrounded by dogs. Her canine companions live in her house, lounging on her furniture and napping under her work desk. The rest of the time, they are well-trained scat-detection dogs that travel around the world on behalf of Working Dogs for Conservation.

Whitelaw acquired Camas as a puppy. Right away, the young German shepherd displayed the two most important traits of a scat-detection dog: a good attitude and an intense drive to chase thrown balls. Whitelaw trained Camas in her backyard, the wide-open spaces near Bozeman, Montana. Over time, the smart black and tan shepherd learned to identify more than a dozen different kinds of animal droppings.

Today Camas leaps over boulders and pushes through the thorny underbrush. She is searching for grizzly-bear scat in the Centennial Mountains that form the Montana-Idaho border.

Nose to the ground, Camas crisscrosses the land, hoping to sniff out the target poop. Alice Whitelaw runs after her fast-moving dog.

After Camas finds the target scat, she gets to play with her favorite ball.

What Kind of Bear Pooped Here?

In one of the first field studies done with the help of wildlife-detection dogs, Samuel Wasser and his teams collected and studied the scat of grizzly bears and black bears in and around Jasper National Park in the Canadian Rockies. The scat of the two bear species look similar, but the dogs knew the difference. Several of the dogs even learned to identify an individual animal. They would sit beside the scat of one specific bear, ignoring all other piles of poop.

Wasser's research revealed that both bear species were seeking out spots beyond the park, specifically on land that had been altered by human activities like logging and road building. For example, the bears gathered to dine on a "salad bar" of clover planted along new roads to prevent soil erosion. Poachers were gunning down these fatter and more visible bears. To protect the bears, the researchers recommended closing some areas to off-road vehicles.

"Go find it!" Whitelaw calls out, over and over. With her nose leading the way, Camas tries to catch a whiff of bear scat in the wind. She races along rough roads, game trails, riverbeds, and ridgelines. After crisscrossing a hillside, Camas stops. She sits and waits until her owner reaches her side and sees the fresh, undisturbed pile of dung.

Whitelaw praises Camas while slipping off her backpack. The dog is patient but wants her reward: a chance to play with her beloved ball. Whitelaw unzips a side pocket and pulls out the ball.

While Camas plays, Whitelaw works. She retrieves a plastic baggy from her backpack and writes an identification number, the date, and the exact location. Next, she turns the bag inside out, and wearing it like a mitten, grabs the scat carefully, not letting it touch anything else. Finally, she rights the collection bag and seals it.

Although the sample will be examined in a laboratory, Whitelaw doesn't doubt her dog's nose. It's grizzly-bear scat. "Camas has been right, always, and she knows it."

The team has more ground to explore. Whitelaw's GPS helps her plot out the area in a grid. She directs Camas to crisscross new sections of the rugged terrain. By the end of the day, Whitelaw's backpack contains more scat samples to help her and others evaluate how this population of bears is doing.

Then it's time to return to base camp. Sometimes camp is a tent in the middle of nowhere. On other trips Camas and Whitelaw sleep in the back of a pickup truck, or if they're lucky, in a dog-friendly motel room. By morning, they are recharged for another day of intensive tracking.

A Backpack Full of Scat

For Alice Whitelaw and other scientists in the field, the day seldom ends at 5 p.m. With luck Whitelaw has a backpack of wild animal poop, which she lugs back to base camp. What she does next depends on where she is staying, the particular kind of scat she has bagged, and the guidelines of the scientific laboratory that will analyze the poop. Whitelaw might freeze the scat so it won't decompose (see below) or put it in ethanol, a clear grain alcohol used as preservative. Sometimes she mixes it with silica gel, little beads that hold and absorb water vapor so the sample won't spoil.

Thanks to Camas and other scat-detection dogs, wildlife experts are piecing together a rough map of where grizzly bears go, and when. This helps them understand bear populations in specific areas, including popular places like Yellowstone National Park, where grizzlies move about in search of food and sometimes interact with people. The data also helps cities and towns plan land use for future generations.

Searching for grizzly scat is vital to the survival of the bears. It's also difficult and dangerous. But at least it's on solid ground.

Left: A log makes a perfect bed!

4 On the Open Sea
Tailing Whales

Samuel Wasser was the first person to use dogs to track scat on the water. He and Barbara Davenport searched for dogs with wide stances that could keep their balance in a rocking boat. They tested candidates for seasickness by taking them for boat rides on a lake.

Then they trained the dogs to find smelly, goopy whale poop.

The Scoop on Orca Poop: Tucker

Since the late 1990s some groups, or pods, of orcas in Washington State's Puget Sound have declined in number. Wildlife biologists want to know why.

Left: Even though he's afraid of water, Tucker leans over the bow to sniff the air. He loves his job!

Orcas are the largest members of the dolphin family.

Gooey green orca scat floats on the water before sinking.

Dr. Wasser trained Tucker, a happy-go-lucky black Labrador-retriever mix, to help locate and gather orca scat. He then turned Tucker over to Liz Seely, the dog's new trainer and handler, after the pair bonded in 2010. Today Seely continues the orca research under Wasser's supervision.

On a working day Seely and Tucker get into a boat and motor into the Sound. Waves rock the hull of the boat, and currents pull at it. Tucker crouches low on the floor of the boat, sniffing for orca poop. Seely's job is to understand her dog's body movements and be aware of the shifting wind. To determine the wind's direction, Seely squeezes baby powder into the air. Soon "the whole boat is white from the powder." When Tucker waves his tail or turns excitedly, Seely signals the captain, wildlife biologist Dr. Deborah Giles, to redirect the boat to follow the changing wind and the compass-like nose of the black Labrador.

Suddenly Tucker hurries to the boat's bow, straining at his leash as though he might leap into the sea—even though he doesn't like to swim. Seely hangs on tight. Her dog smells orca poop! Dr. Giles snakes the vessel back and forth until they find the stinky source, which is "bluish-green-black and gooey like snot." They quickly scoop up the slimy blob in a net before it sinks.

Tucker has spent more than two thousand hours on the research vessel. He has located over five hundred samples of poop that have been flushed out of the digestive system of orcas in Puget Sound. The scat gives scientists an amazing treasure trove of information that tells them the age, sex, and identity of each killer whale. Scientists also learn what the animal is eating and if it is healthy or stressed.

The numbers of orcas are declining, but they are not listed as an endangered species . . . yet. Scientists are racing to find out why they are disappearing.

Could orcas be dying because of chemical pollution? Some groups of orcas have the highest PCB levels of any **mammal** in the world. This man-made chemical is often found in plastic products, electrical equipment, and oil. PBDE, a flame retardant, is also in the orcas' body tissues. Industrial activity around Seattle may leach these toxic chemicals into the water.

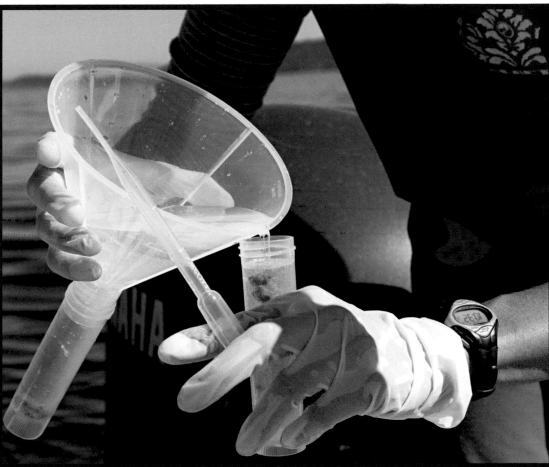

After the scientists scoop the poop, they prepare samples of it at the back of the boat.

A Whale of a Tale: Gator

Gator, a chunky Australian cattle dog, used to sniff for illegal drugs with Washington's Department of Corrections. Drug-sniffing dogs always work on a short leash, and usually in busy, noisy public places like train stations and airports. The dogs must pay 100 percent attention to their handlers all of the time. For some dogs it can become too exhausting.

Gator needed to make a career change, so he went to the Center for Conservation Biology to learn how to track down the scat of wolverines, fishers, bobcats, pumas, bears, and lynxes. He still follows commands, but he can run freely over large wilderness areas and often be leash free.

Gator is also a pro at finding floating feces at sea. When his body goes stiff, his mouth opens, his ears tip forward, his tail goes straight up, and his nose twitches, everyone knows that an orca has pooped nearby!

Could the orca population be declining because of noise pollution? Each summer, whale-watching boats pursue orcas and other large mammals in Puget Sound. The Navy also conducts regular underwater explosions in the Sound. Noise from the boat motors and the explosions appears to bother orcas and many other marine mammals that use **sonar**. The noise makes it harder for the animals to use sound waves to hunt, navigate, or communicate with one another.

Chemical pollution and noise pollution do seem to be problems for the orcas. But based on the scat Tucker has helped collect, Dr. Wasser believes that the change in the orcas' population is related to a drastic decline in their main food source—Chinook salmon. There are fewer fish due to overfishing, **global warming**, and dams that block the salmon from leaving the ocean and swimming upriver to their spawning grounds.

The natural life cycles of the orcas and the salmon are both out of balance. Thanks to the scat-sniffing noses of Tucker and other detection dogs, Wasser and others know why, but they need to find solutions, and quickly.

Finding the Right Whale: Fargo and Bob

Meanwhile, on the other coast of North America, super sniffers are helping scientists study critically endangered North Atlantic right whales. These slow-moving, fifty-ton mammals feed in waters off New England and Canada between July and October. They give birth to calves near the southeast coast of the United States between December and March.

In the 1800s, right whales were hunted to near extinction for their oil and baleen, a fibrous material in their mouths that filters their food. Today fewer than five hundred of these gentle giants survive. Time is running out for the right whales, and they are the subject of an intense research and conservation effort.

Fargo, a big, ball-loving Rottweiler, is part of that effort. Once a narcotics-detection dog and then a grizzly-poop tracker, Fargo teamed up with Dr. Rosalind Rolland from the New England Aquarium in Massachusetts to try something totally new.

Wearing a brightly colored vest and using his super-sensitive nose, Fargo sniffs for the smelly, bright orange poop of the North Atlantic right whale from the bow of a boat. Thanks to his sharp nose, scientists have been able to collect and test three hundred samples of whale poop. No wonder they nicknamed him "Whale Dog"! Fargo has one problem: he gets seasick, so Dr. Rolland, who is also a veterinarian, gives him motion-sickness pills to settle his stomach.

Bob, a Beauceron mix, is also helping in the effort to save the North Atlantic right whale. But the first time Bob met a right whale up close, the terrified dog dove to the bottom of the boat. The whale was more than twice the size of the boat! Now Bob is comfortable sniffing for whale poop. He, Fargo, and other dogs can locate whale scat more than four times as fast as humans, and from farther than one nautical mile (a little more than one land mile) away.

If detection dogs can find scat on land and at sea, what's next? What other **conservation targets** can they sniff out with their incomparable noses?

Training Whale Dogs

For whale dogs like Fargo, Tucker, and Bob, training begins on land. Small bits of frozen poop are placed in mason jars. Each dog must learn to find the scat of a specific species of whale, and nothing else.

The next phase is at sea. Dog and handler go out in one boat. About a half-mile away, a researcher on another boat sets out bits of whale scat in a floating box or bowl. Using its sense of smell, the dog must find the floating samples. The captain of the boat and the dog's handler watch as the dog turns and wiggles from head to tail to indicate the direction of its find. Following the dog's cues, the boat moves slowly toward the sample.

Eventually the team heads farther out into the frigid ocean to find the target whales—like this breaching North Atlantic right whale.

5 Beyond Poop
Finding Tortoises, Turtle Eggs, and Owl Pellets

Sometimes it's more effective to train a dog to find an actual animal, a freshly laid egg, or even a ball of owl barf instead of a pile of poop!

Low and Slow: Desert Tortoises

Alice Whitelaw and her dogs, including Camas, drive south to California's Mojave Desert. Whitelaw comes prepared for the desert environment. Her dogs might wear a heat-reflective cape in the sun, or booties over their paws to protect them from cactus thorns and burning rocks and sand.

The team is here to find desert tortoises, a federally listed **threatened species**. Most of the time the tortoises stay in underground burrows in the sand. In the early mornings and late afternoons of summer, the tortoises leave their burrows

Left: A juvenile desert tortoise pauses beside a beavertail cactus in bloom.

Look What Came in the Mail!

Today we can ship almost anything in the mail, including cotton swabs that have been rubbed on living tortoises to capture their smell. When these swabs arrive in Alice Whitelaw's mailbox in Montana, she opens the precious package carefully. She uses the samples to train her dogs to identify the scent of a desert tortoise. Then it's time to head out into the field!

Camas and Alice Whitelaw have found a desert tortoise.

to eat plants and find mates. They move slowly on their short, stumpy legs.

Adult desert tortoises can grow to about fourteen inches in length, but they're difficult to spot because their mottled shells match their surroundings. Tortoise hatchlings are tiny—about the same size as your big toe! Camas and other detection dogs are able to "air scent" even the smallest tortoises, based on scent carried on wind currents.

As Camas sniffs under rocks and plants, Whitelaw watches and listens for rattlesnakes, which are also active on warm days. She makes sure her dogs get water, and lots of it. Without enough water the dogs will dehydrate and lose energy. If they get overheated and pant too much, they can't smell as well.

Now Camas sits beside what at first looks like a small rock. It's a young tortoise, with a thin, fragile shell. As the dog waits patiently, Whitelaw records the location of the tortoise on her GPS and measures the animal's shell.

If there are numerous tortoises in a section of desert, then federal, state, and

Camas's sharp nose leads her to this teeny hatchling. A ballpoint pen provides a size comparison.

local experts need to sit down together. They discuss the future of the desert tortoise in that location. Maybe it isn't the best place to build a new golf course or highway. Should builders move their project somewhere else? Maybe the tortoises are in the middle of a practice bombing range used by the US Air Force. Should the tortoises be relocated to a safer spot in the desert? If so, where and how?

Camas and other dogs are doing their part to help answer these difficult questions.

One Smart Puppy: Ridley

When Ridley was a puppy, Donna Shaver and Stephen Kurtz trained him by hiding treats around their home. At first Ridley looked, more than sniffed, for the treats. Shaver had to remind him to use his nose. Next she taught the dog to identify the smell of turtle eggs. Within ten weeks Ridley was a pro, racing down the beach at the command of "Go find the nest."

Sand Flippers: Kemp's Ridley Sea Turtles

All five sea-turtle species found in the Gulf of Mexico are listed as threatened or endangered. The Kemp's ridley sea turtle is the rarest.

Since 1978 the United States and Mexico have worked side by side to save the species from extinction. One of the most effective conservation sites is at Padre Island National Seashore in Texas, where Kemp's ridley sea turtles nest between April and mid-July. Females crawl out of the surf, dig a nest, and lay clutches of about one hundred eggs. Using their hind flippers, they bury the soft, white eggs in the sand. Then they return to the sea.

During the nesting season, experts search daily for the eggs. They walk or drive up and down the beach, hoping to find turtle tracks. No one wants the eggs to fall prey to raccoons or coyotes, or wash away during high tide. But it's a difficult task. Winds blow some tracks away, and tides wash away others.

That's when it's time to bring in Ridley, a Cairn terrier with a powerful nose and an independent spirit. He belongs to Dr. Donna Shaver, director of sea-turtle recovery on Padre Island, and her husband, Stephen Kurtz.

Ridley sniffs for turtle eggs—specifically, the mucus-like fluid coating them. When he catches that smell, he alerts his handlers by sitting still. No one doubts Ridley. They carefully dig up the sand next to him and find the hidden turtle eggs.

Later in the summer the eggs hatch, and tiny gray hatchlings no bigger than large buttons emerge. When they are released on the beach, the hatchlings know instinctively to crawl to the ocean and swim away.

Will the Kemp's ridley sea turtle survive? Donna Shaver and others believe that saving every single egg could mean the difference between extinction and a comeback.

Left: Donna Shaver moves sand aside to uncover the eggs that Ridley detected.

Right: The delicate eggs are packed in an insulated box and rushed to a temperature-controlled incubation building.

Winged Wars: Northern Spotted Owls

The northern spotted owl has become a symbol of conservation.

Several thousand pairs of spotted owls are scattered throughout the Pacific Northwest, where they live and nest in old-growth forests of large, ancient trees. The shy, big-eyed owls are very territorial, and their numbers decline dramatically when their habitat is disturbed.

The 1980s saw a national clash between loggers, who wanted work, and conservationists, who wanted to save the owls by preserving old-growth forests. There were demonstrations and protests, lawsuits and court cases. After the northern spotted owl was listed as a threatened species in 1990, a federal court closed much of the Northwest woods to logging. Logging essentially shut down.

Despite all of this, spotted owls are now vanishing faster than ever. Scientists have a **hypothesis**—an idea based on facts—about what may be causing the problem, but to prove it, they need to do their homework.

Like all owls, spotted owls vomit up balls of indigestible rodent fur and bones. These owl pellets land under trees in the dark, dense forest. Researchers at the Center for Conservation Biology depend on Max and other detection dogs to find them.

Jennifer Hartman fell in love with Max, an Australian cattle dog, the moment she first saw him in 2009. With his pointy ears and his tri-colored coat, he reminded her of a miniature wolf or coyote. Hartman became Max's primary trainer and handler at the Center for Conservation Biology. Since then, they have worked on many projects, including the search for spotted owls.

The morning sunlight filters through the canopy as Max and Hartman hike through the forest. Suddenly Max goes into alert. Hartman looks up. Four owls—two juveniles with their parents—perch on a tree limb. The ground is littered with their pellets.

Max knows he's made a good find. He prances around the tree as Hartman pulls out his ball, and then waits eagerly for her to toss it in his direction.

Dog teams also gather pellets from barred owls that have settled into what has traditionally been spotted-owl territory. Barred owls bother spotted owls, take over their nests, and sometimes even eat them. They are bigger and meaner than their cousins, and they can easily adapt to a new area. As scientist Dr. Dominick DellaSala says, "They are the new bully on the block." After barred owls move in, the spotted owls seem to vanish.

Max alerts Jennifer Hartman that there are owl pellets nearby. Does he know that an owl dozes above him?

A handler swabs an owl pellet for DNA.

Scientists are analyzing the pellets of both birds. They hope to learn how many owls live in the forest, what they are eating, and how healthy the birds are. Maybe they'll discover why the barred owls are relocating. Is the move related to **climate change**? Or is it just a natural expansion of the barred owls' territory?

ooo

The use of working dogs to assist scientists in the field is rapidly expanding as super sniffers learn to locate much more than poop: they can now track down live animals, eggs, urine, hair, and more. These skills are indispensable in the race to save endangered animals. They are also critical in the fight against **invasive species**.

Sometimes science is done sitting on the forest floor. In this case, two handlers from the Center for Conservation Biology process owl pellets.

Sniffing for Plants

For dogs, plants are trickier to smell than animals or scat. According to Dr. Deborah Woollett, co-founder of Working Dogs for Conservation, "Plants have a more scattered scent . . . more smeared, more diffused." David Vesely of the Oregon Wildlife Institute says searching for plants is mentally hard for dogs—a bit like a human doing math problems for hours.

Vesely owns and handles Rogue, a Belgian sheepdog whose job is to locate Kincaid's lupine in the shrinking prairie of Oregon's Willamette Valley. Kincaid's lupine is a threatened **native** prairie plant that is host to the endangered Fender's blue butterfly.

In search of lupine, Rogue scrambles up the steep hills and jagged ridges where the plants thrive. He pushes through knee-high prairie grass and prickly bushes. Then he slows to circle one spot, stops, and sits. Beside him is a dark, leafy plant. It's Kincaid's lupine.

6 Invasion!
The Hunt for Harmful Insects, Snails, and Snakes

Tiny insects are sucking the life out of California's grapevines. Cannibal snails are preying on Hawaii's native snails. Burmese pythons are strangling and swallowing small mammals in Florida's Everglades National Park. Across the country, destructive species are invading new habitats and upsetting the balance of nature. Canine detectives are trying to stop them.

Bug Off! Rixi on the Run

On a beautiful fall day, Rixi, a German shepherd, leaps out of a truck and runs into a vineyard. He dances around Shay Cook, co-founder of Insect Detection Dogs in California. He barks and barks!

"Sit, Rixi," Cook commands. "Bug, Rixi, bug."

What does Rixi smell?

Left: Canine detectives like EcoDogs Jake and Ivy are sniffing out invasive Burmese pythons in the Florida Everglades.

Risky Work

Is this a safe job for Rixi? Or for his handler, Shay Cook? Not necessarily. They won't run into a grizzly bear—but the fields may have been sprayed with harmful pesticides or other chemicals. There could be hidden rat or gopher traps, or even rattlesnakes.

Following each daylong field session, Cook peels off her protective jumpsuit and washes her shoes. She hoses Rixi down, too.

Off Rixi streaks, racing up and down rows of grapevines with his nose in the air. He is seeking a specific smell: the **pheromone** of a female vine mealybug. Females release the scent to attract males or leave messages for other mealybugs.

The vine mealybug is a pest in Mediterranean countries and other warm regions around the world. In the United States it is harming California's multibillion-dollar grape industry. It infests the vine, damages the fruit and leaves, and makes the grapes unmarketable. Rixi is a mealybug's worst enemy. He can cover more ground in a day than a crew of field workers can in several days.

Today the athletic brown and black shepherd searches sixteen acres in the first hour. Each acre is about the size of a football field. All of a sudden Rixi jams to a stop next to a vine and barks excitedly. Sure enough, under the vine's bark hides a single mealybug—just one eighth of an inch in length.

Cook doesn't remove the bug. While Rixi prances about with his rope toy, she flags the vine and records its location on her GPS. The vineyard owner must decide what to do next. Perhaps he'll remove the vines in that area, or just spray that particular plant with pesticide.

After some water and rest, Rixi returns to work, racing up and over a series of hills. Cook is just as fit as her dog, but it is still hard to keep up with Rixi.

Cook and other dog handlers say there's no question that a canine can be trained to detect the distinct smell of many kinds of insects. Already, beagles sniff for the scat of wood-boring beetles in woodpiles and in living hardwood trees like maples. Other dogs are being trained to find biting bedbugs, destructive termites, and other harmful insects.

Trouble in Paradise: Cannibal Snails

Millions of years ago plants and animals began to populate the Hawaiian Islands. Over time there **evolved** some 750 species of native snails found nowhere else in the world. Today fewer than one hundred species remain, due to habitat loss and invasive **predators** such as rats and rosy wolf snails.

The rosy wolf snail was introduced to Hawaii in 1955 in an attempt to control other exotic snails. The plan backfired: the rosy wolf snail nearly decimated the native snail population. Nicknamed "cannibal snails," these two- to three-inch-long snails eat other snails, slugs of all kinds, and even each other. They are considered one of the world's worst invasive species.

In the **rain forests** of Hawaii, native, now-endangered tree snails dine on algae growing on leaves, helping to maintain the trees' health. The rosy wolf snail follows the tree snail's slime trail and often swallows the smaller snail in one gulp. The wolf snail's pink tissue is clear enough that you can see the prey slip down the esophagus into the stomach.

Tree snails reproduce at a true snail's pace. They begin having offspring when they are about four years old and then have only a few each year. Rosy wolf snails are eating them faster than they can reproduce.

At home in Montana, handlers at Working Dogs for Conservation used rosy wolf snails imported from the islands to train Wicket, Tsavo, and Tia. When Wicket and the other dogs got to Hawaii, they searched the rain forest for the invasive snails. Unfortunately the dogs weren't able to discover any more snails than the humans. More training is in order for these hard-working canines!

Wicket sniffs a rosy wolf snail. It's hard for dogs to find these targets because snails don't give off much of an odor.

Too Many Pythons: Ivy and Jake in the Everglades

Dr. Christina Romagosa grips a captured Burmese python in Florida's Everglades.

Many years ago pet owners began dumping their unwanted, fast-growing Burmese pythons into Everglades National Park. Today the native species in the park are disappearing, but not the pythons. Instead, the snakes are thriving! With no natural predators, the snakes are devouring rabbits, birds, and even small alligators. They are also reproducing quickly. One of the biggest captured pythons in the park was 17 feet long, weighed 164 pounds, and was pregnant with 87 eggs.

Canine detectives Jake and Ivy are on the case. Back at EcoDogs headquarters in Alabama, handlers trained the Labrador retrievers to locate snakes hidden in sacks in a field.

Now Jake, Ivy, and their handlers head out into the Everglades, searching canal banks, marshy areas, and grassy fields for pythons. Jake is unusual because he uses both "ground scenting" and "air scenting" skills. Sometimes he runs along with his nose skimming the ground, following the old, slithering trail of a python. Most of the time, though, he and Ivy hold their noses up. They zigzag back and forth, changing direction when the wind shifts. Finally tails wiggle and bodies squirm with excitement. Jake and Ivy smell a python. But where is it?

Good find, Jake!

The dogs circle the area, growing more and more excited as the smell of snake gets stronger. Suddenly Ivy and Jake pause and sit; they have found the python. The handlers don't see the snake at first. Then they spot the large, well-camou-flaged **reptile** dozing in the sun just a dozen feet away.

Taking a Break

It's important that Ivy and Jake rest, especially in the steamy Everglades. "These dogs work incredibly hard. They love what they're doing," EcoDogs co-founder Todd Steury says. "They just work to the point of exhaustion and we actually have to force them occasionally to stop and take breaks." But taking a break doesn't mean that Ivy or Jake can jump into the nearest pond or waterway to cool off. It might mean death for the dogs if they encounter a hungry alligator or python.

Ivy and Jake have done a good job! They are each rewarded with a rubber Kong, a bouncy toy filled with treats. Then the dogs rest in the shade while the handlers capture the strong, squirming snake and slip it into a mesh bag. Data collected from the snake will help park staff find ways to reduce the population of these invasive predators.

Everyone is pleased with Jake and Ivy's work. Over several months in the field, they and other detection dogs prove two and half times more likely to find a python than human researchers—and twice as fast.

Using trained dogs to hunt for conservation targets and invasive species is a new and fast-growing field. Local, state, and federal agencies are hiring these elite canine teams to assist with research projects in the United States and Canada. In recent years, dog teams have also been traveling around the world to help save the planet's most endangered animals.

It's much easier to hang on to a powerful python after it's secured in a bag.

Shiver and Shake

A female Burmese python lays her eggs (up to one hundred) in March or April. To keep the eggs warm, she wraps herself around them and continually contracts and relaxes her muscles. This constant shivering movement warms her coils by several degrees above air temperature. When the babies hatch two to three months later, they are about twelve to eighteen inches long and ravenous. Babies and mother head out separately to hunt for food.

To help control the python population, research teams remove clutches of eggs like the one shown above.

7 Frequent Flyers
Finding Scat Around the World

Meet the Energizer Dog: Pepin

Pepin, a Belgian Malinois, is hyper-focused. He has flown around the world to track the scat of cheetahs, African wild dogs, snow leopards, and other endangered animals.

Pepin was trained by his owner and handler, Dr. Megan Parker of Working Dogs for Conservation. Parker set out jars of different kinds of scents, including snow-leopard scat sent to her from Mongolia. When Pepin finally smelled the jar containing snow-leopard scat, he went wild.

Whatever he does, Pepin gives it 110 percent. He acts like he has had too much coffee most of the time! But Pepin can somehow turn off his high-energy switch and stay calm when he works as an international ambassador for Working Dogs for Conservation—or when people pet him at local events in his hometown of Bozeman, Montana. He loves playing "horsey" and other games with children.

According to the Center for Biological Diversity, our planet is in the midst of a major extinction of plants and animals. Extinction this massive hasn't occurred since the loss of the dinosaurs sixty-five million years ago. Some scientists estimate that 30 percent or more of all species will disappear within the next few decades. That's why finding solutions now is critical!

It takes the combined help of volunteers, scientists, governments, parks, preserves, universities, and conservation organizations around the world. Everyone has the same goal: to determine the fragile status of endangered plants and animals before it's too late. Using scat-detection dogs to assist efforts beyond North America's borders is new, but they are already providing valuable data.

Left: Up, up, and away! Lily, Wicket, and their handlers, Aimee Hurt and Tyler Rhody, pose for a quick photo before flying.

Metal Detector on Four Paws

Poaching, a multibillion-dollar business, is the illegal trapping, hunting, and killing of wild animals for a profit. One tiger carcass—meat, bones, organs, and especially the skin—fetches thousands of dollars. Poachers are relentlessly pursuing tigers, elephants, lions, rhinos, gorillas, and other wildlife populations.

Some poachers place a circular steel trap called a snare along a trail. When stepped on, the snare tightens around an animal's body or foot. The snare is wired to the ground so the poacher can come kill the animal and take tusks, horns, or other parts to sell.

Talented super sniffer Wicket hunts for snares in Zambia in Africa. With her amazing sense of smell, she can actually find the metal. The snare is destroyed so it cannot be used again. Aimee Hurt hopes these efforts by Wicket and other detection dogs slow down the poachers.

Jet Setters: Dogs on the Go

Traveling outside the United States with a dog team requires lots of planning. Handlers need tickets, passports, and permits for the work they are going to do. Since they often go to remote spots, they need to know about the availability of veterinarians in case the dogs need emergency medical care. They pack lots of protein-rich dog food, a water-purification system, protective canine clothing like booties, and toys. Because detection dogs are not service dogs like Seeing Eye dogs, they must fly with the luggage in travel crates. The dogs need layovers for walks, meals, and bathroom breaks, so an overseas trip requires many stops.

Wildlife biologists and handlers also pack special clothing for themselves, such as sun hats with netting, and extra medication, such as pills to prevent malaria (a disease carried by mosquitoes). Sometimes the team needs camping equipment, too. Dog and handler might have to travel by car, boat, bus, train, propeller plane, or even helicopter to reach their destination. They could be going to a hot, dry desert, a steamy jungle, or a rugged mountain range.

Move over, Max! You can't drive this snowmobile!

Where Have All the Tigers Gone?

On silent, padded paws, tigers prowl alone in search of deer, pigs, and buffalo to satisfy their large appetites. These wide-ranging carnivores can survive in habitats from rain forests to grasslands to snowy mountains in India and many other Asian countries.

Tigers are solitary and shy, making them difficult to study.

Unfortunately thousands and thousands of acres of land are being carved up for human development, destroying the tigers' natural habitat. That makes the tigers easier targets for farmers protecting their livestock and for poachers illegally hunting the big cats. In 1920 some one hundred thousand tigers lived in the wild; today that number is in the low thousands. According to some conservation organizations, tigers face possible extinction in the wild by 2030.

Desperate scientists and conservationists are turning to canine detectors for help.

In many Asian countries, no one has seen evidence of tigers for years. The Center for Conservation Biology is trying to help change that, partnering with the World Wildlife Fund on its Global Tiger

Initiative project in Cambodia. Jennifer Hartman and Liz Seely traveled with Max and black Labradors Sadie May and Scooby Doo to the northeast corner of the country, where the World Wildlife Fund manages a few protected forests. Elephants carried their gear into the jungle, and dogs and people camped out together for twelve days at a time. Hartman and Seely were to determine the number, if any, of tigers, leopards, and wild dogs in the area.

According to Hartman, the team collected hundreds of scat specimens. None were from tigers, but the data helps the World Wildlife Fund assess the possibility of the big cats someday returning to those protected forests. Hopefully the information will tell scientists if there is enough natural food and fresh water there for the tigers' comeback.

Gathering data is part of a ten-year, multimillion-dollar program to try to increase tiger populations throughout Asia and Russia's Far East. Creating a plan is a complex, ongoing project, but detection dogs are helping conservationists understand the present—and future—of these critically endangered animals.

Aimee Hurt and Wicket are ready to go—on an elephant!

Can the Cross River Gorilla Be Saved?

The Cross River gorilla was thought to be extinct until 1980, when a lone animal was spotted. It is now considered the most endangered of all the apes in Africa. There are probably a few hundred individuals left in the wild, living in small groups along the rugged border of Cameroon and Nigeria.

Cross River gorillas reproduce slowly, with females having babies only every four or five years. They also need a sizable territory, as they are always on the move in search of fruit and other plant foods.

But like tigers, gorillas are losing their homeland to **deforestation**. Farmers cut down native plants the gorillas eat and replace them with crops. Another problem is the possible transmission of diseases and parasites among people, livestock, and gorillas. Cross River gorillas have also been hunted by poachers, making them extremely wary of humans.

In 2011, Working Dogs for Conservation teams traveled to Cameroon to help wildlife managers gain a more accurate population estimate of these secretive animals. Everyone worked hard! In Kagwene

This Cross River gorilla, one of the last of her kind, lives at the Limbe Wildlife Centre in Cameroon.

On the jungle floor Aimee Hurt prepares samples of what she hopes is Cross River gorilla dung.

Gorilla Sanctuary and Mone River Forest Reserve, detection teams bagged more than three hundred scat samples. Most would have been impossible to find without sharp-nosed Wicket, Lily, and Orbee.

Canine Ambassadors

"Village dogs" are common in many African communities. Since they don't get fed regularly, the dogs hover near cooking centers for bones and scraps of meat while growling and snapping at one another. They are generally untrained and act wild. Used to these dogs, many Africans were at first wary of Wicket and the other canine detectives. But it didn't take long for them to reach out and pet them—and to step in as handlers when necessary.

Aimee Hurt says that in some of the small settlements, "seeing a couple of white women and three big dogs was really big news. The . . . kids [were] intrigued." She impressed the children "by playing fetch with Lily for a while."

Wearing flashy red vests that read "Search Dog," the super sniffers even visited a school. The children learned about the Cross River gorillas that still live in their surrounding mountains. Many had never before thought about what the term "endangered species" might actually mean.

A Super Team of Super Sniffers

Before Orbee, Wicket, and Lily became a team, they were rescued and trained by Aimee Hurt at Working Dogs for Conservation. Orbee, who was raised to herd cattle and failed at that job, was redirected to find the tiny scat of blunt-nosed leopard lizards in the United States and gorilla dung in Africa. Lily, a yellow lab mix, was passed on to five different homes because she was too energetic and intense to be a pet. Now her long tail seldom stops wagging because she has a job she enjoys. Since being adopted and trained by Hurt, Wicket has traveled some fifty thousand miles around the world.

At last it was time for the children to pet a dog, some for the very first time. Everyone touched one, even though it was terrifying for many. Orbee loved leaning against the schoolchildren for ear rubs and rolling on his back for belly scratches. Students in Cameroon still ask about Wicket, Lily, and Orbee, proving that detection dogs are amazing ambassadors for conservation wherever they go.

For Wicket, Lily, and Orbee, it was just another enjoyable workday.

Left: Camp tender William plays with Wicket, Lily, and Orbee.

Conclusion
It's a Dog's Life

Training and caring for a dog is expensive. So is transporting a canine-detection team to a faraway work site. Most of the groups that work with wildlife-detection dogs—Working Dogs for Conservation, the Center for Conservation Biology, and EcoDogs—are **nonprofit organizations**. Their goal is to benefit the general public: not to make a profit, but to exist for charitable or educational purposes. They rely on grants, donations, and funding from private and public groups to make their work possible.

Left: Retirees Lulu and Shrex vacation in California's Sierra Nevada.

Wherever they work—in Phnom Penh, Cambodia, in this case—handlers need a lot of gear for themselves and their dogs.

Just One Poop Can Change the World

Pepin earns smiles and pats from fans in Myanmar.

There are only a handful of wildlife-detection-dog organizations in the United States. They are all busy! But it's not just about research in the field. Conservation education is also part of these groups' mission. Every group educates the public about what they do and why. For example, it's important for everyone to know that elephants are dying at the hands of poachers who want their tusks. The Center for Conservation Biology relies on social media, printed articles, television, radio interviews, and teacher's packets to get the word out. High school students in Washington, for instance, learn about the techniques used by scientists to extract DNA from scat and analyze it.

Of course, some of the most effective ambassadors are the dogs themselves. The dogs and their handlers go into the communities where they are working to give demonstrations and inform the public. Many people know about dogs that catch criminals and sniff for drugs and bombs. But they usually aren't familiar with the work of scat-detection dogs.

The Golden Years: Retirement

For every canine detective there is a time to retire. How long a dog can work depends on the specific animal. Most dogs work up to the age of eight or nine. Some older dogs cut back on their work hours or are used to train new handlers. Others completely retire from active duty. Handlers must decide for them, since a typical detection dog is all heart, often pushing beyond his or her physical capabilities.

All the retired dogs from Working Dogs for Conservation continue to live with their trainers. For Aimee Hurt and Alice Whitelaw, their dogs have earned the opportunity to lie in the sun, stretch out on the furniture, or saunter with them on a walk.

Handlers at EcoDogs and other canine-detective organizations are often allowed to adopt the dogs they've trained and worked with in the field. Some of Samuel Wasser's dogs live at the Center for Conservation Biology for their remaining years. The rest of them find forever homes. After years of fieldwork they are often more mellow and ready to become a pet. Potential families are carefully screened, and the dogs are not released until they are matched with the perfect family.

Many of the heroic detection dogs in this book are retired or have changed jobs. EcoDogs's Ivy retired from her work with pythons and was adopted by a loving family; her partner, Jake, switched jobs to sniff for newborn fawns and deer antlers in Alabama. Bob, the whale-tracking Beauceron mix, retired to a farm in Vermont.

The First Poop Detective

Moja, the first scat-detection dog trained by the Center for Conservation Biology, worked with Dr. Wasser tracking grizzlies and black bears in Canada. For many years Moja starred in magazine and newspaper articles, and was even on television. Then he retired and lived happily with Wasser. Several years later, Moja died of heart failure, but his legacy—of proving that scat-detection dogs can do the job—opened up an entirely new and noninvasive approach to conservation biology.

Ridley the Cairn terrier still lives with Donna Shaver and her husband. He helps find the most difficult-to-locate turtle nests. In his free time, he enjoys walking, eating, napping, and barking so that great blue herons do not land in his yard.

Wicket and Aimee Hurt, her handler, have traveled to seven countries for Working Dogs for Conservation. Nowadays, Hurt wants Wicket to keep working, but closer to home. The "crazy" rescue dog is still as playful as ever. Some mornings, she wakes her sleeping canine housemates by barking. Thinking that someone is coming into the house, the other dogs rush to the front door. Wicket quickly settles down on the best, cushiest bed for a nap.

Tucker, the orca-poop sniffer, is still a sailor from May to October. The rest of the year, the seventy-five-pound black Labrador takes it easy with his handler and trainer, Liz Seely.

Max and Scooby Doo still work with Jennifer Hartman. If Hartman is in the field with only one dog, the other goes to the kennel at the Center for Conservation Biology. The rest of the time, the dogs live with Hartman. The three take daily trips to the grocery store, as well as trips to more exotic spots, such as Alaska.

Max even visits schools! Hartman hides a

Scooby Doo enjoys some quiet time.

sample of orca-whale scat in the classroom, and the children watch Max sniff the air until he finds the hidden sample. Hartman saves all the thank-you cards and pictures children mail to Max.

Paw Prints on Our Hearts

Some of the dogs in this book have died, or as some owners like to say, "gone over the rainbow." Fargo the gentle Rottweiler tracked the scat of many species, but he is most famous for being a whale dog. He died in 2010 at the age of ten. Gator the Australian cattle dog tracked the scat of orcas and other animals for the Center for Conservation Biology. He lived happily with his trainer, Heath Smith, until his death in 2013.

After nine years of detection work, Camas retired a few weeks before her thirteenth birthday. According to Alice Whitelaw, the German shepherd deployed on twenty-five different projects involving thirteen different scent targets, including grizzly scat. She could locate live animals like the desert tortoise, and plants, too. Whitelaw published numerous scientific reports, thanks to Camas's detection work.

Until her death in 2011, Camas was always "vocal, growling, and barking." "[She let] us know what she want[ed] when she want[ed] it," Whitelaw says, "a scratch on the butt, her ball, food, or someone to fill the water bowl." Clever Camas could also be sassy. "She [was] hilarious and [knew] it," remembers Whitelaw, "which made for years of laughter while working with her in the field."

RIP Camas, 1997–2011

Of the many conservation detection dogs that have retired or passed on, Megan Parker of Working Dogs for Conservation writes, "We give thanks to them, for their contribution to science and conservation, and mostly for their ability to bring so much to each of us." It's a fitting tribute. What could be better than working with dogs like Fargo, Camas, and Wicket, experiencing their work ethic and dedication to the task?

Lily and her friend Fatty take a break to play tug-of-war.

The accomplishments of the Center for Conservation Biology, Working Dogs for Conservation, EcoDogs, and other similar organizations reflect their amazing dogs, hard-working trainers, and dedicated wildlife specialists. Scat detection is a new field with promising results. This is only the beginning. In the decades ahead, species around the globe will have a chance to renew and survive, thanks to the tireless work and spirit of these super sniffers and all those who love them.

Detection dogs are all heart!

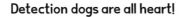

Author's Note

I observed Dr. Vickers (left) and Dr. Boyce evaluate this undersized bobcat on a dark, cold night in the desert. It gave me great respect for the work they and other scientists do.

My family lives part-time in the Anza-Borrego Desert in Southern California. Our one-room house is five miles to the nearest town, and the road is unpaved for half that distance. All around us lie thousands of acres belonging to Anza-Borrego Desert State Park.

Our neighbors include several University of California, Davis, wildlife veterinarians who research desert animals. One night Drs. Walter Boyce and Winston Vickers came to dinner and talked about their work trapping mountain lions and bobcats and fitting them with radio collars in order to track and study them. They discussed the challenges of trapping and tranquilizing wild cats, including the physical danger to the animal.

"What's the alternative?" I casually asked, and with that question, I was introduced to the world of scat-detection dogs. Twenty-four hours later, after being glued to my computer to learn more, I was hooked and began to envision a book. The rest is history!

When I started this book, all the detection dogs I studied were actively working in the field. Since then some have retired; others have passed on. Because each dog's story is special, and because I want my readers to feel right there with these amazing stars, I chose to write their stories in the present tense.

Freddie's story in the introduction is not based on any one dog, but on many I read about during my research. He represents what happens when a seemingly untrainable dog is rescued, retrained, and given a second chance.

Acknowledgments

During the research and writing of this book, I communicated with many amazing people—dog handlers, volunteers, wildlife biologists, researchers, graduate students, and wildlife veterinarians. All gave freely of their time and patiently answered my many questions. I thank them all! Including Walter Boyce and Winston Vickers, they are:

- Bonnie Brown-Cali, owner of Dog Dynamics
- Dr. Mary Cablk, associate research professor of biology at Desert Research Institute
- Shay Cook, co-founder of Insect Detection Dogs
- Jennifer Hartman, canine handler at the Center for Conservation Biology
- Aimee Hurt, co-founder and director of operations at Working Dogs for Conservation
- Elizabeth Seely, canine handler at the Center for Conservation Biology
- Dr. Donna Shaver, chief of sea-turtle science and recovery at Padre Island National Seashore
- Heath Smith, lead trainer and coordinator at the Center for Conservation Biology
- Dr. Todd Steury, co-founder and science liaison at EcoDogs, Detection Dogs for Ecological Research
- Dr. Samuel Wasser, director of the Center for Conservation Biology
- Alice Whitelaw, co-founder and director of programs at Working Dogs for Conservation

While researching and writing this book, I was especially inspired by *Dog Heroes of September 11th* by Nona Kilgore Bauer. Working dogs are heroes in my mind, and I thank them for putting their lives and hearts on the line for us.

Jennifer Hartman gives Max a drink from a portable water bowl. Staying hydrated in the field is all-important for both dog and handler.

What's in a Handler's Pack?

rainproof notebook and markers

water purifier

emergency blanket

pocket knives

scat-collection bags

binoculars

food for handler

dog safety vest

harmonica

backpack

dog working harness

floating dog toy

collar and leash

handler safety vest

dog goggles for boat or snow

headlamp

insulated dog jacket

dog brush

dog cooling jacket

water bottles

dog boots and liners

GPS devices, radio, cell phone, compass, and spare batteries

watertight container for cooling jacket

first-aid kit

waterproof box

dog toys

bear bell

bear repellent

collapsible water bowl

Photo Credits

Poop by any other name—dung, feces, excrement, scat—is still poop! This is Bengal tiger poop.

Glossary

air scent: To pick up smells carried by the air.

alerting: When a dog sits or lies down to signal to its handler that it has made a find.

balance of nature: The stable state in which natural communities of plants and animals coexist.

canine: A dog or doglike mammal.

canine handler: The human who takes care of a dog and directs its activities.

carnivore: A meat-eating animal.

cell: The smallest basic unit of a living thing. Each cell has a job: the smell-receptor cells in the nose, for example, detect tiny particles of scent in the air.

climate change: A change in weather patterns that lasts for a long time.

conservation target: An animal or plant that humans are trying to protect.

data: Information.

deforestation: The removal of trees from a forested area.

DNA: Short for deoxyribonucleic acid, the material in a cell that determines a living thing's genetic characteristics (inherited traits).

dung: See *scat*.

endangered species: A species that has a high risk of extinction in the near future. Protected plants and animals are on the US government's Endangered Species List.

evolve: To slowly change over generations.

excrement: See *scat*.

extinction: When a species no longer exists anywhere on earth.

feces: See *scat*.

Global Positioning System (GPS): A navigation system that uses signals from space-based satellites to provide location information.

global warming: The rise of the average air, land, and water temperatures on earth.

habitat: The home environment of an animal or plant.

hypothesis: In science, an idea or explanation that is based on known facts but that has not yet been proven.

indicating: See *alerting*.

invasive species: A species living outside its normal habitat that disrupts the balance of nature in a region.

mammal: A warm-blooded vertebrate (animal with a backbone) that has hair or fur and produces milk for its young.

native: Occurring naturally in a specific habitat.

nonprofit organization: A business that is not intended to make money.

olfaction: The process of smelling.

parasite: An organism that lives on or in another living thing. Parasites do not benefit their hosts—and can often harm them.

pheromone: A smell that is released by an animal to signal other animals of the same species.

poaching: The illegal hunting of animals.

predator: An animal that hunts other animals for food.

prey: An animal that is hunted by other animals for food. To prey on means to hunt and eat another animal.

rain forest: A dense forest that gets at least one hundred inches of rain each year.

reptile: A cold-blooded, scaly vertebrate (animal with a backbone).

scat: Solid waste material eliminated by an animal. Also called dung, excrement, feces, or poop.

scenting: When a dog searches for and identifies a specific smell.

sonar: The use of sound waves to detect objects underwater or in the air.

species: A specific type of animal or plant.

target animal: An animal that is the subject of research.

territory: The area that an animal occupies. A territorial animal defends its home.

threatened species: A species that has a high risk of extinction in the future. Plant and animal species that are on the US government's Threatened Species List are closely watched so they don't become endangered.

Tia gets some up-close instruction from handler Alice Whitelaw.

Pepin races toward his target.

Resources

Books

Castaldo, Nancy. *Sniffer Dogs: How Dogs (and Their Noses) Save the World*. Boston, MA: Houghton Mifflin Harcourt, 2014.

Dell, Pamela. *Surviving Death Valley: Desert Adaptation*. Mankato, MN: Capstone, 2008.

Holland, Jennifer S. *Unlikely Heroes: 37 Inspiring Stories of Courage and Heart from the Animal Kingdom*. New York: Workman Publishing, 2014.

Patent, Dorothy Hinshaw. *Super Sniffers: Dog Detectives on the Job*. New York: Bloomsbury, 2014.

Stamper, Judith Bauer. *Eco Dogs*. New York: Bearport Publishing, 2011.

Websites

Center for Conservation Biology: **www.conservationbiology.uw.edu/**

EcoDogs: **www.vetmed.auburn.edu/research/cps/**

PackLeader Dog Training: **www.packleaderdogtraining.net**

Padre Island National Seashore: **www.nps.gov/pais/**

Ridley Ranger on Facebook: **www.facebook.com/Ridley-Ranger-167512136595629**

Working Dogs for Conservation: **www.wd4c.org**

Working Dogs for Conservation on Facebook: **www.facebook.com/WorkingDogsForConservation**

Quotation Sources

Max sprawls on the grass, enjoying a day off from work.

For more information about the sources below, please see the bibliography on pages 77–78.

Introduction

Page 6: "The dog needs . . . curious spirit": Alice Whitelaw, quoted in Etter.

Page 6: "win the game": Randy Gross, quoted in Bauer, p. 56.

Page 6: "They're obsessive-compulsive . . . 24 hours a day": Katherine Ralls, quoted in Nelson.

Chapter 1

Page 12: "You can get . . . single animal": Samuel Wasser, quoted in Meadows, p. 24.

Page 13: "Guru of Doo-Doo": Nelson.

Chapter 2

Page 18: "If the wind . . . a circle, too": Samuel Wasser, quoted in Meadows, p. 25.

Page 18: "to be able . . . to accomplish": Aimee Hurt, quoted in MacKay.

Page 19: "She'll wait quietly, . . . before her turn": Aimee Hurt, quoted in Socie.

Page 19: "pungent enough . . . from a distance": Sakariassen.

Page 20: "the possibility . . . find scat": Todd Steury, quoted in Lacey.

Pages 20–21: "They looked . . . can do it'": Todd Steury, quoted in Lacey.

Page 21: "24–7 endeavor. . . . to retirement": Aimee Hurt, quoted in Sakariassen.

Page 21: "the love . . . their leashes": Aimee Hurt, quoted in Bauer, p. 18.

Chapter 3

Page 25: "Go find it!" Alice Whitelaw, quoted in Sakariassen.

Page 26: "salad bar": Samuel Wasser, quoted in Nelson.

Page 26: "Camas has been . . . knows it": Alice Whitelaw, quoted in Etter.

Chapter 4

Page 30: "the whole boat . . . powder": Samuel Wasser, quoted in Sutherland.

Page 31: "bluish-green-black . . . snot": Samuel Wasser, quoted in Weir, p. 21.

Deborah Woollett of Working Dogs for Conservation puts Orbee through his paces in the field.

Chapter 5

Page 38: "Go find the nest": Donna Shaver, quoted in Guthrie.

Page 41: "They are . . . the block" Dominick DellaSala, quoted in Welch.

Page 43: "Plants have . . . more diffused": Deborah Smith (now Woollett), quoted in Raff.

Chapter 6

Page 45: "Sit, Rixi" and "Bug, Rixi, bug": Shay Cook, telephone interview with author, November 7, 2011.

Page 50: "These dogs work . . . take breaks": Todd Steury, quoted in Lacey.

Chapter 7

Page 58: "seeing a couple . . . for a while": Aimee Hurt, quoted in Working Dogs for Conservation newsletter, March 8, 2012.

Conclusion

Page 62: "Just one poop can change the world": Paraphrase of "Just one fox poop can change the world," from Working Dogs for Conservation newsletter, n.d.

Page 65: "vocal, growling, and barking": Alice Whitelaw, quoted in Working Dogs for Conservation newsletter, December 2010.

Page 65: "[She let] us . . . the field": Alice Whitelaw, quoted in Working Dogs for Conservation newsletter, December 2010.

Page 66: "We give thanks . . . each of us": Megan Parker, quoted in Working Dogs for Conservation newsletter, December 2010.

Selected Bibliography

In addition to the sources listed below, I also relied on information from personal interviews, conducted in person, by phone, or by email, with Alice Whitelaw, Aimee Hurt, Todd Steury, Samuel Wasser, Elizabeth Seely, Jennifer Hartman, Donna Shaver, Mary Cablk, Shay Cook, and Heath Smith.

Bauer, Norma Kilgore. *Dog Heroes of September 11th: A Tribute to America's Search and Rescue Dogs*, 10th anniversary ed. Freehold, NJ: Kennel Club Books, 2011.

Braatvedt, Julian. "Working Dogs for Conservation." Vimeo video, 2014. https://vimeo.com/92590065

Etter, Lauren. "Scratch 'n' Sniff Special Canine Unit Knows to Nose Scat." *Wall Street Journal*, September 23, 2006. http://www.wsj.com/articles/SB115897478418372106

Guthrie, Andrew N. "Ranger Ridley." *The Bark*, May/June 2009.

Kwok, Roberta. "Cool Jobs: Delving into Dung." *Science News for Kids*, January 23, 2013. https://student.societyforscience.org/article/cool-jobs-delving-dung

Lacey, Derek. "EcoDogs: Auburn's Detection Dogs for Ecological Research." *The Corner News*, July 24, 2011. http://www.oanow.com/the_corner_news/article_8f0bc077-6c8a-571b-ab95-7da292032b2d.html

MacKay, Paula. "Conservation Dogs Work for Wildlife." *The Bark*, Fall 2005. http://www.thebark.com/content/conservation-dogs-work-wildlife

Meadows, Robin. "Scat-Sniffing Dogs." *Zoogoer*, September/October 2002, 22–27.

Morell, Virginia. "Animal Minds." *National Geographic*, March 2008, 36–61.

Nelson, Bryn. "Dogs Have a Nose for Doo-Doo." NBC News.com, November 30, 2007. http://www.nbcnews.com/id/21980526/ns/technology_and_science-innovation/t/dogs-have-nose-doo-doo/#.VRB0BPnF89I

Ridley scans the sand for the scent of buried turtle eggs.

Best buddies Wicket and Aimee Hurt enjoy a view in Szechuan, China.

Parker, Megan. "Right Under Our Noses—Dogs are Saving the World." YouTube video, 12:05. Posted by TEDx Talks, March 27, 2013. https://www.youtube.com/watch?v=MYJd-HysnRI

Potter, George, and Eric Bendick. "TERRA 236: Working Dogs—On Nature's Trail." Life on Terra video, 2006. http://lifeonterra.com/terra-236-working-dogs-on-natures-trail/

PBS Kids Go! "Real Scientist: Aimee Hurt." PBS Kids: DragonflyTV video, Twin Cities Public Television, 2007. http://pbskids.org/dragonflytv/scientists/scientist61.html

Raff, Lily. "Science Goes to the Dogs." *The Bulletin*, June 29, 2008. http://www.bendbulletin.com/news/1464389-151/science-goes-to-the-dogs

Sakariassen, Alex. "Conservation's Best Friend." *Missoula Independent*, May 28, 2009. http://missoulanews.bigskypress.com/missoula/conservations-best-friend/Content?oid=1148006

Socie, Kathryn. "Sniffin' Out Scat for Conservation." *High Country News*, November 12, 2007. http://www.hcn.org/issues/358/17345

Sutherland, Amy. "Dogs Sniff Out Whale Scat." *The Bark*, July/August 2009. http://thebark.com/content/dogs-sniff-out-whale-scat

Swain, Glenn. "Canine Conservationists on the Move." *New York Times*, September 5, 2012. http://green.blogs.nytimes.com/2012/09/05/canine-conservationists-on-the-move/?_r=0

Wasser, Samuel. "Lucky Dogs." *Natural History*, October 2008, 48–53.

Weir, Kirsten. "Dog Chases Whale Scat." *The Scientist: Magazine of Life Sciences*, August 2006, 21.

Weiss, Kenneth R. "A Nose for Wild Things." *Los Angeles Times*, November 13, 2010.

Welch, Craig. "The Spotted Owl's New Nemesis." *Smithsonian*, January 2009. http://www.smithsonianmag.com/science-nature/the-spotted-owls-new-nemesis-131610387/?c=y%3Fno-ist

West Paw Design. "Working Dogs for Conservation Field Demo." You Tube video, 2011. https://www.youtube.com/watch?v=cWa8rrNJZDY

Index

Sampson stays up late reading a novel about a brave, bold Labrador. If only this were true!